FULL STEAM BASEBALL

Science, Technology, Engineering, Arts, and Mathematics of the Game

by N. Helget

CAPSTONE PRESS
a capstone imprint

Fact Finders Books are published by Capstone Press
1710 Roe Crest Drive, North Mankato, Minnesota 56003
www.capstonepub.com

Library of Congress Cataloging-in-Publication Data
Names: Helget, Nicole Lea, 1976– author.
Title: Full STEAM baseball : science, technology, engineering, arts, and mathematics of the game / by N. Helget.
Description: North Mankato, Minnesota : Capstone Press, 2019. | Series: Fact finders. Full STEAM sports | Audience: Age 8–14.
Identifiers: LCCN 2018016135 (print) | LCCN 2018019614 (ebook) | ISBN 9781543530469 (eBook PDF) | ISBN 9781543530384 (hardcover) | ISBN 9781543530421 (pbk.)
Subjects: LCSH: Baseball—Juvenile literature. | Sports sciences—Juvenile literature. | Sports—Technological innovations—Juvenile literature.
Classification: LCC GV867.5 (ebook) | LCC GV867.5 .H444 2019 (print) | DDC 796.357—dc23
LC record available at https://lccn.loc.gov/2018016135

Editorial Credits
Editor: Nate LeBoutillier
Designer: Terri Poburka
Media Researcher: Eric Gohl
Production Specialist: Kris Wilfahrt

Photo Credits
AP Photo: Bizuayehu Tesfaye, 27, Charles Rex Arbogast, 17, Reed Saxon, 14; Dreamstime: Glen Jones, 26, Laurence Agron, 20; Getty Images: Adam Glanzman, 18, Al Tielemans, 21, David E. Klutho, 7, Matthew Stockman, 22, Robert Beck, 10, Simon Bruty, 9, Tom DiPace, 8, Transcendental Graphics, 25, Walter Iooss Jr., 15; iStockphoto: 33ft, 4; Library of Congress: 24; Newscom/Icon Sportswire: John Cordes, cover, Juan DeLeon, 29, Tony Quinn, 13; Shutterstock: Frank Romeo, 23

Design Elements
Shutterstock

Printed in the United States 6367

CONTENTS

INTRODUCTION

A CHANGING GAME

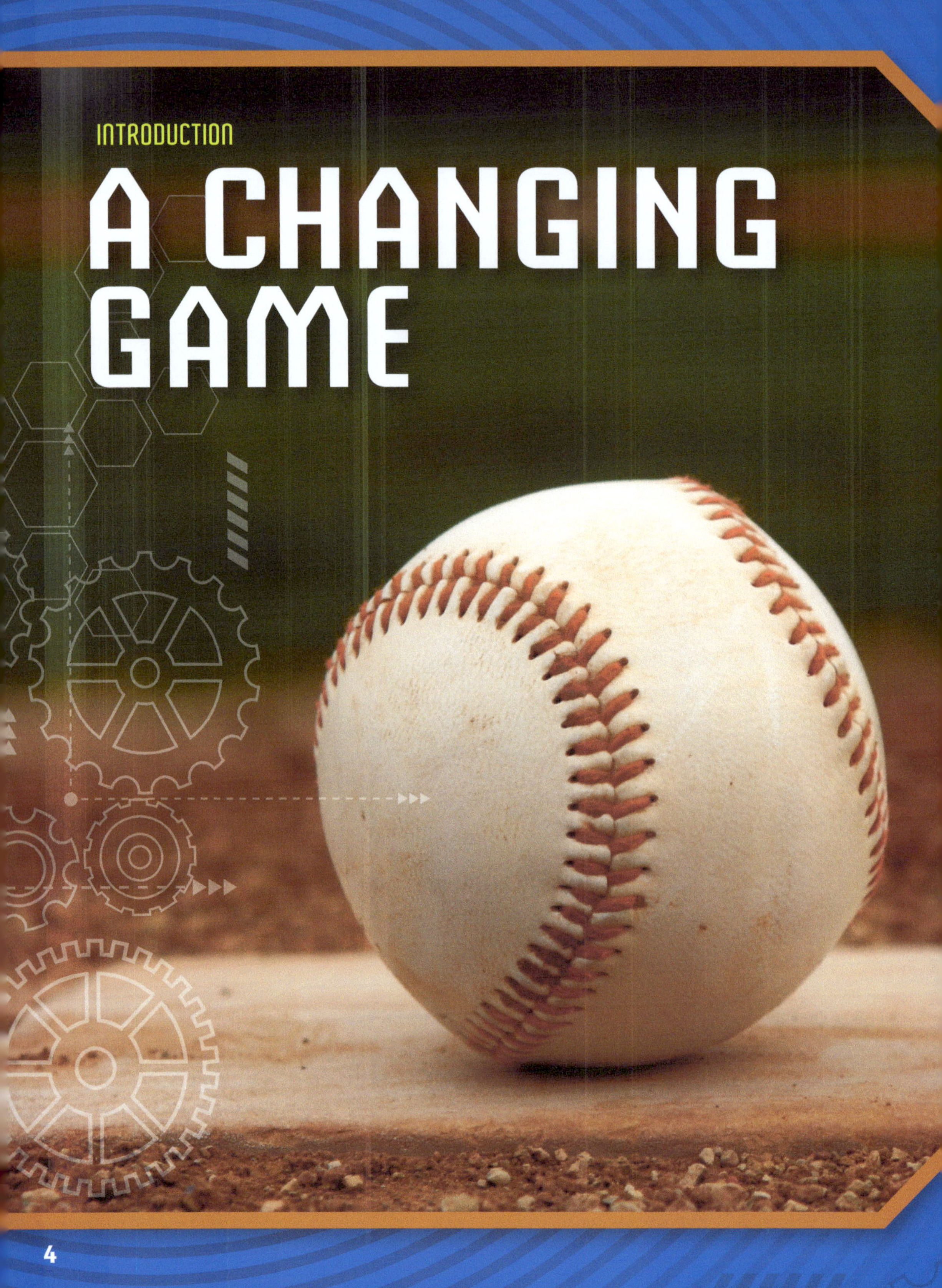

The popularity of baseball in America rose in the 1860s. Back then players needed only a ball, a bat, and an open field. Coaches and players soon made the sport more competitive. Play improved. The equipment got better too. Infielders started wearing homemade buckskin mittens or leather mitts padded with cotton. Companies changed the designs of balls, bats, and gloves. More recently video recordings and computers have impacted the game. Let's look at how science, technology, engineering, the arts, and mathematics (STEAM) come together to make the sport what it is today.

CHAPTER ONE

SCIENCE

BIOMECHANICS: How Do Pitchers Throw?

Did you know there's science behind a pitcher's throw? It is called biomechanics, the study of how bodies move. To pitch, or throw the ball to a batter, the pitcher goes through a series of steps.

The first step is the wind-up. The pitcher raises his hands together, turns to the side, and lifts his knee.

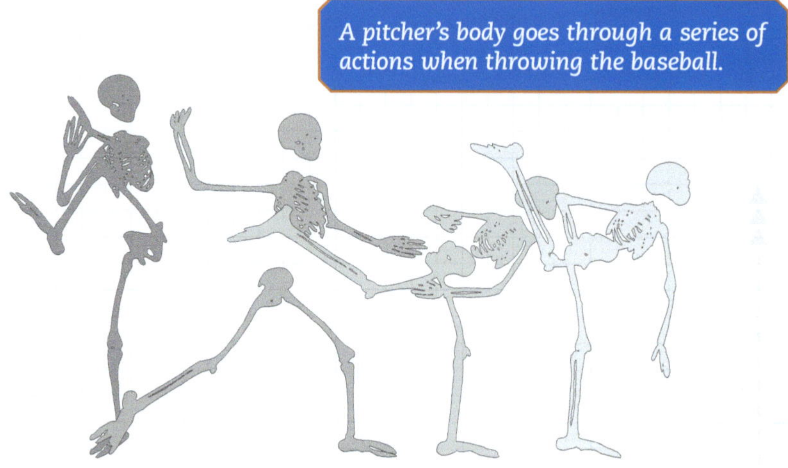

A pitcher's body goes through a series of actions when throwing the baseball.

Pitcher Clayton Kershaw cocks his arm before throwing the ball over the plate.

The next steps happen quickly. In the stride, the pitcher moves his front leg forward toward home plate. He cocks his arm behind his head in the next step. Then the pitcher whips his arm down, letting the ball go. The **force** of his arm movement gives the ball forward momentum. Finally, having let go of the ball, the pitcher brings his leg down. His arm comes to a stop across his body.

force—an act that changes the movement of an object

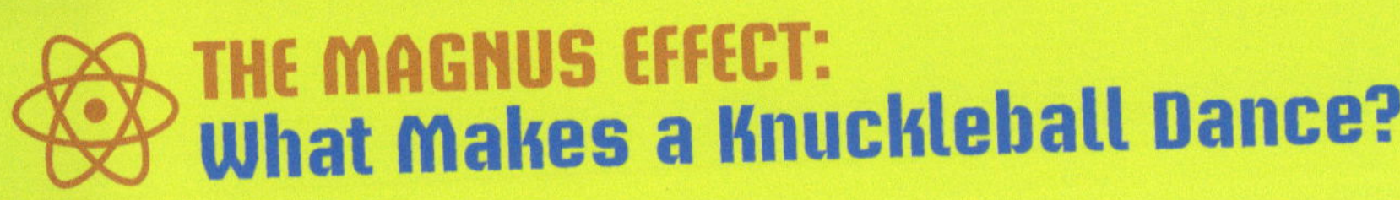

THE MAGNUS EFFECT: What Makes a Knuckleball Dance?

The pitcher throws the ball. He has no idea exactly where the pitch will go. He's thrown a pitch called a knuckleball. This pitch may wobble or float in any direction as it "dances" over the plate. For a knuckleball to dance, it has to *avoid* something called the **Magnus effect**.

A curveball is a pitch that experiences the Magnus effect. When the spinning baseball flies toward the plate, it creates two layers of pressure. There is a high-pressure layer of air. It is on the side of the ball that's spinning in the direction the ball's traveling.

A pitcher grips the ball with his fingertips to throw a knuckleball.

R.A. Dickey used his knuckleball to have a great 2012 season. He led the National League in strikeouts.

On the other side of the ball, there is low pressure. The high-pressure air causes a force on the low-pressure side of the ball. The force causes the ball to curve away from its straight line of flight.

To throw a knuckleball, pitchers grip the baseball with their knuckles or fingertips. They balance it with their thumb. When they let go of the ball, the pitchers *push* it away from their hand. This prevents spinning. The ball floats toward home plate with little rotation.

Magnus effect—a force produced by differences in air pressure around a spinning object

EXIT SPEED AND LAUNCH ANGLE: The Home Run Swing

Here comes the pitch. It dips toward the outer corner of the strike zone. The batter shifts his weight to his back leg and swivels his hips. His bat slices over the plate.

His bat connects with the ball. In the instant when the ball and the sweet spot on his bat collide, he feels nothing. The energy of his swing has been perfectly transferred to the energy of the pitch. He hears a familiar *CRACK*! That ball is out of here.

Power hitter Albert Pujols captured National League Most Valuable Player honors in 2005, 2008, and 2009.

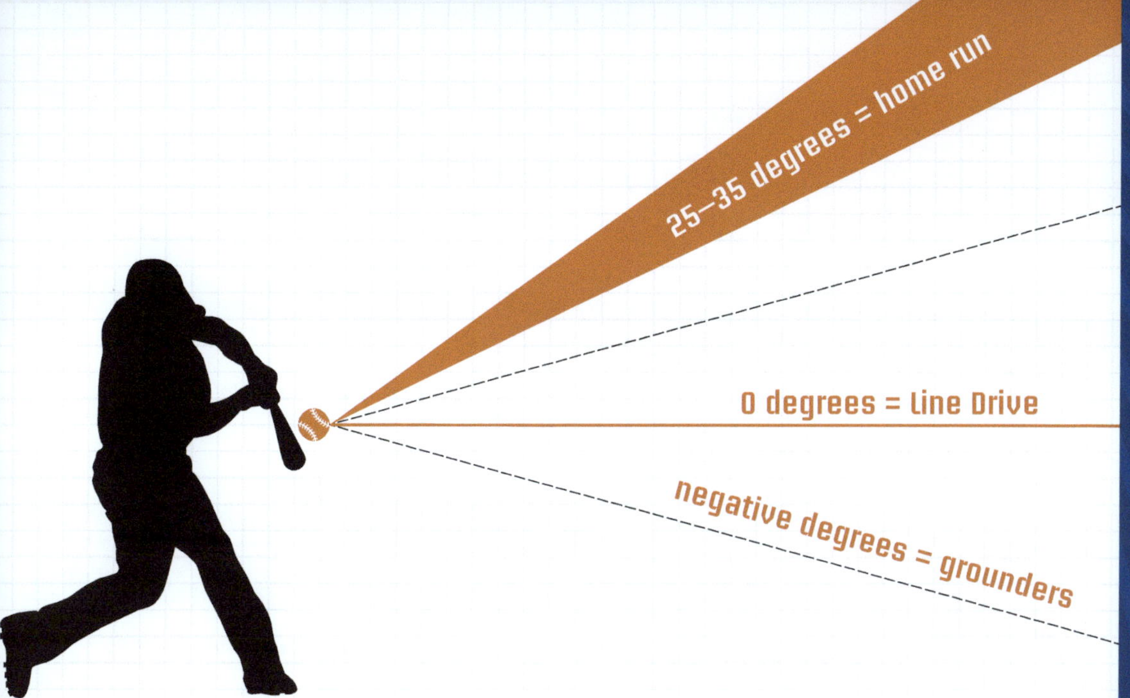

The home run equation is **exit speed** plus **launch angle**. Exit speed measures the **velocity** of the ball's flight off the bat. An exit speed of more than 90 miles per hour is home run territory. But that's only true if the launch angle is correct too. Launch angle refers to flight of the ball after it connects with the bat. A flat launch angle of zero degrees equates to a line drive. Negative launch angles produce grounders. Positive launch angles are fly balls. The home run launch angle is around positive 25 degrees.

exit speed—the speed of a baseball after it is hit by a batter

launch angle—the angle at which a baseball ball leaves a player's bat after being struck

velocity—the speed and direction of a moving object

CHAPTER TWO

TECHNOLOGY

COMPUTERS AND SOFTWARE: Instant Replay

Before **instant replay** technology, baseball calls were left entirely to the umpires' judgment. Other pro sports already used replay technology. But many people argued that instant replay would make the game of baseball even longer than it already was. Major League Baseball (MLB) games last two to four hours, or even longer.

The Washington Nationals and the Chicago Cubs squared up for the National League Division Championship in 2017. Neither team could have guessed instant replay would impact the outcome of their game.

instant replay—a recording of an action in a sports event that can be shown on video immediately after the original play happens

In the 8th inning, the Nationals had tying and go-ahead runners on second and first base. The Cubs' catcher threw to the first baseman to try to snag the runner off the bag. The runner slid back as the first baseman applied the tag. It looked close. The umpire called "safe." But the Cubs disagreed. After instant replay review, the umpires decided the first baseman had applied the tag in time. The call was reversed. The Nationals' rally was over. The Cubs went on to win the game. The game lasted more than four and a half hours.

Instant replay allowed umpires to review the Cubs' Anthony Rizzo's tag on the runner.

MEDICAL ADVANCEMENTS: Tommy John Surgery

The stress of pitching can cause injury to a pitcher's arm. Before 1974 a torn ulnar collateral **ligament** (UCL) was a career-ending injury. But thanks to the understanding of biomechanics and the skill of surgeon Dr. Frank Jobe, pitchers have a new option.

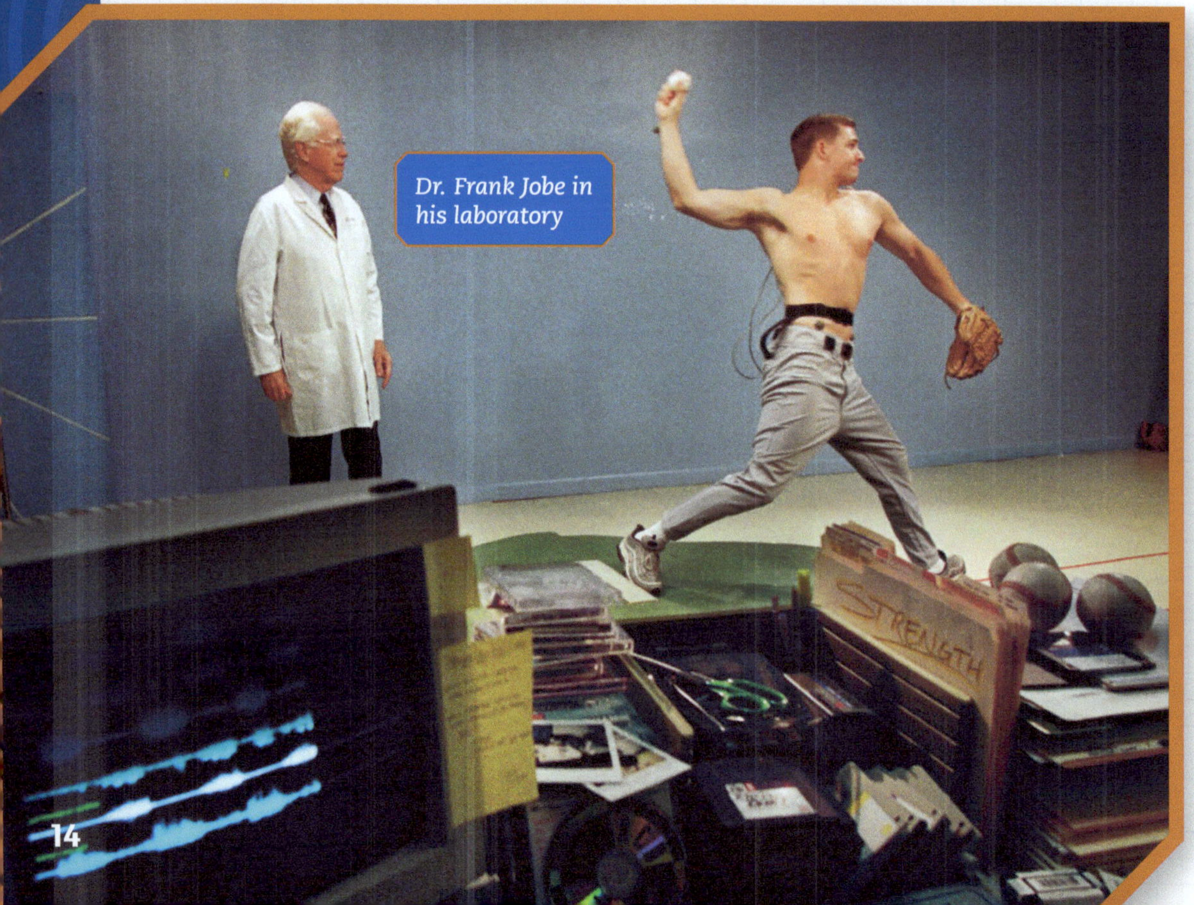

Dr. Frank Jobe in his laboratory

Jobe worked with the Los Angeles Dodgers. The ways in which pitchers treated their aching elbows—with ice, heat, and homemade chicken skin rubs—got Jobe's attention. He wondered if there was a better way.

Tommy John pitched 26 seasons in the major leagues.

The surgery to repair a damaged UCL is named for the first pitcher it was performed on, lefty Tommy John. In 1974 Dr. Jobe took a **tendon** from John's healthy right arm and put it in John's left arm. After recovering, John added 14 more seasons to his pitching career. The surgery has improved since then and is more common. Today nearly one-third of MLB pitchers have had Tommy John surgery.

ligament—a band of tissue that connects or supports bones and joints

tendon—a strong, thick cord of tissue that joins a muscle to a bone

BATTING PRACTICE: A Smarter Swing

Pro players today grew up practicing their swings on batting tees and pitching machines. Thanks to technology the science of the swing has changed.

Scientists and manufacturers came together to build the "Smart Bat." The Smart Bat looks like a regular bat. But the bat has a sensor inside. It tracks the hitter's velocity, angle, and power. The data is sent to a computer or a smart phone.

Hitters also use **virtual** batting cages. A hitter steps inside the cage and sets up to swing. The technology works like a Wii Sports video game. The pitch comes in from a screen. The hitters digitally smack curveballs and crush fastballs on the outside corner. They can practice hitting different pitches. Those "hits" appear on a digital field. It shows how far the player hit the ball and where. Coaches and managers study the information. It's used to make batting lineup decisions before a game.

A virtual reality headset and a plastic bat let players practice their swings.

virtual—existing or occurring on computers or on the Internet

CHAPTER THREE

ENGINEERING

MATERIALS: The Making of the Wooden Bat

Hitters wear gloves to get a better grip on the wooden bat.

A major league rule says bats used in games must be made of wood. The bat can't be longer than 42 inches. The barrel can't be bigger than 2.75 inches around.

Most bat-makers use ash trees as the raw material. At the mill, only the best logs are chosen. A mill worker cuts the logs into sections called splits. A cutting machine called a lathe shaves off the rough bark. That section of wood is called a billet. Workers carefully examine every single one. They pick the billets with the straightest grain and paint the ends so the wood won't rot. The billets are left to dry for six months to two years.

When a billet is dry, it is made into the shape of a baseball bat. It's skinny on the grip end and fatter on the barrel. Then the bats are sorted according to weight. Next the bats go to bat turners. They sand the bats and measure them. When it's just right, the bat has the company's brand put on it.

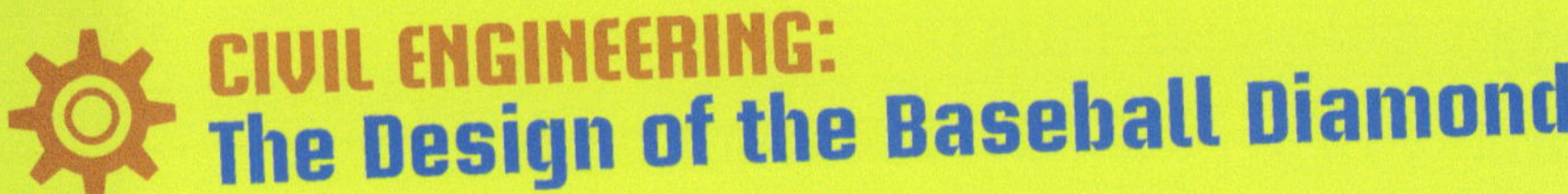

CIVIL ENGINEERING: The Design of the Baseball Diamond

Civil engineers design, build, and maintain roads and buildings and everything in between. They even play an important part in designing baseball fields. When planning a baseball field, engineers study how to work with the landscape. The infield is dug out and made level. The outfield might be designed to have a natural or manmade slope.

The Toronto Blue Jays play their home baseball games at Rogers Centre.

Before each game, the grounds crew use chalk to outline baselines and the batter's box.

Algebra matters in field design too. Home plate is the anchor upon which every other base, the pitching rubber, and the foul poles are measured. After home plate is placed, second base is measured from the back corner of home plate to exactly 127 feet and 3 3/8 inches. From the view of the catcher, a baseball field looks like a diamond. The infield is, in fact, a perfect square. There's 90 feet from home plate to first. There's 90 feet at a 90 degree angle from first to second and so on.

algebra—a branch of mathematics that uses numbers and letters that represent numbers

CHAPTER FOUR

ARTS

ARCHITECTURE: Two Stadium Stories

In 1965 the Houston Astros had a problem. The ceiling panels of the newly-built Astrodome made it nearly impossible for outfielders to spy fly balls. The panels reflected the indoor lights. Rays of sunlight shone in players' eyes. Routine pop-ups turned into dropped balls. The ceiling was soon painted white. While the paint helped the players, it stopped sunlight from reaching the grass. Within weeks the grass died. Artificial turf was installed. But the fake grass caused injuries. Players said it smelled bad too.

The Houston Astrodome was home to the Astros until 2000.

Target Field opened in 2010 in Minneapolis.

Today architects work to design better stadiums. In 2006 the Minnesota Twins and the city of Minneapolis began planning a new baseball stadium. They thought about the environment. They wanted the new stadium to have as little of an impact on the environment as possible. The stadium is designed so that rainwater is collected. It's then reused to wash the seats. The stadium also takes part in a recycling program that turns its waste into energy.

THE ARTS: Cartoons and Baseball

Newspapers and magazines have run stories about baseball since the 1800s. Often cartoons were printed alongside the stories.

Famous cartoonist Gene Mack worked for *The Boston Globe* during the Great Depression. Many people during this time were without jobs. Baseball was one way people could have affordable fun.

Babe Ruth played for the New York Yankees from 1920 to 1934.

This baseball cartoon appeared on a magazine cover in 1895.

The New York Yankees offered star player, Babe Ruth, an $80,000 salary. Fans were shocked. Most of them would never see that much money in their lifetime, much less in one year. The U.S. president didn't even make that much.

Gene Mack showed the public's shock in a famous cartoon. Titled "Is Babe Ruth Worth It?," one boy says to another, "Of course the Babe ought to get more than the president . . . did [President] Hoover ever get 60 homers in one year?" The simple cartoon made a big point.

CHAPTER FIVE

MATHEMATICS

STATISTICS: Box Scores and Sabermetrics

A **box score** is one way to tell the story of a game. The box score lists **statistics**, or stats. It includes players' names and positions, along with their number of at-bats, runs, hits, RBIs, extra base hits, steals, sacrifices, and errors. A box score also shows scoring by inning, and lists pitchers who appeared, along with their innings pitched, hits, runs, walks given up, and strikeouts.

Baseball fan Bill James took interpreting stats in pro baseball games to a new level. He was curious and asked questions about baseball players. He wondered how often the lead-off batter scored if he reached first base. He wondered what the statistics showed if a closing pitcher threw every game versus taking a break between games.

James argued that too much value went to earned run average (ERA) and batting averages, which are simple equations. He thought managers overvalued those two stats and wondered whether there wasn't more to be explored in the numbers. What about on-base percentage? What about slugging percentage? What about if a player is on a "hot streak"? Turns out there was a lot more to explore. By analyzing **quantitative** data from all aspects of the game, eventually known as "**sabermetrics**," coaches were able to strategize better and win more games.

Bill James

box score—the printed score of a game, giving names and positions of players and statistics

statistic—a fact shown as a number or percentage

quantitative—of or relating to how much there is of something

sabermetrics—studying statistics from baseball games in order to review and compare the performance of individual players

QUANTITATIVE DATA: In Fielding

A fielder's performance was once measured mainly by counting **errors**. But this measurement couldn't record a hit-stealing catch.

Mathematicians now use a sabermetric called Wins Above Replacement (WAR). This number shows a player's overall contribution to the team. It includes the player's ability to keep the other team from scoring runs. It also counts how he helps his own team score runs. To do the calculation for a fielder, you use six data points. They cover all the ways a player can help or hurt their team. There is no one way to calculate the WAR. Many mathematicians use computer programs.

(Batting Runs + Base Running Runs + Fielding Runs + Positional Adjustment + League Adjustment + Replacement Runs) / (Runs Per Win) = WAR

error—when a defensive player makes a mistake while fielding the ball

Andrelton Simmons of the L.A. Angels had the highest defensive WAR in the league in 2013, 2014, and 2017.

A high WAR means that a player adds value to the team. A low WAR means he is playing worse than a similar player. This stat might be helpful in a tough situation. A manager with an open position can use the WAR to decide which player to put in.

Fans learn the stats of star players and study the throws of ace pitchers. Baseball fans learn even more when they think about how science, technology, engineering, the arts, and mathematics (STEAM) affect their favorite sport.

GLOSSARY

algebra (AL-juh-bruh)—a branch of mathematics that uses numbers and letters that represent numbers

box score (BOKS SKOR)—the printed score of a game, giving names and positions of players and statistics

exit speed (EG-zit SPEED)—the speed of a baseball after it is hit by a batter

error (ER-ur)—when a defensive player makes a mistake while fielding the ball

force (FORS)—an act that changes the movement of an object

instant replay (IN-stuhnt ri-PLAY)—a recording of an action in a sports event that can be shown on video immediately after the original play happens

launch angle (LAWNCH ANG-guhl)—the angle at which a baseball leaves a player's bat after being struck

ligament (LIG-uh-muhnt)—a band of tissue that connects or supports bones and joints

Magnus effect (MAG-nuhs uf-FEKT)—a force produced by differences in air pressure around a spinning object

quantitative (KWAHN-tuh-tate-iv)—of or relating to how much there is of something

sabermetrics (SAY-bur-MET-riks)—studying statistics from baseball games in order to review and compare the performance of individual players

statistic (stuh-TISS-tik)—a fact shown as a number or percentage

tendon (TEN-duhn)—a strong, thick cord of tissue that joins a muscle to a bone

velocity (vuh-LOSS-uh-tee)—the speed and direction of a moving object

virtual (VUR-choo-uhl)—existing or occurring on computers or on the Internet

READ MORE

Braun, Eric. *Baseball Stats and the Stories Behind Them: What Every Fan Needs to Know.* North Mankato, Minn.: Capstone Press, 2016.

Editors of Sports Illustrated Kids. *Big Book of WHO Baseball.* New York: Sports Illustrated, 2017.

Morey, Allan. *Fantasy Baseball Math: Using Stats to Score Big in Your League.* North Mankato, Minn.: Capstone Press, 2017.

INTERNET SITES

Use FactHound to find Internet sites related to this book.

Visit www.facthound.com

Just type in 9781543530384 and go.

INDEX